meet me at golden hour

by jennae cecelia

meet me at golden hour

meet me at golden hour.
it's so much better here.

my hope for you as you read is that
you will feel warmth and comfort
like the sun and the breeze.

meet me at golden hour is a poetry book
filled with hope on the horizon while also
recognizing that some things in life are brief
and not guaranteed. which is why it is so
important to soak up the moment and be
present.

love,
jennae

meet me at golden hour

life's too short to
not paint with your fingers,
sing that song at the top of your lungs,
eat your favorite ice cream
on the last day of summer,
or dance in the kitchen as pancakes bake.
your inner child would thank you
for not taking your life too seriously.
this life's supposed to be fun.

i want the nine at night sun
in the summer
when it's winter and i forget
what it feels like to not be
left in the dark so early.

i'm probably too loud for you.
that part i know to be true.
but i won't settle my wind,
or silence my rustling leaves
to give you the quietness you want.
just so you can be the only one
heard or not.

i've always been a little lost.
directions aren't my thing.
i'm trusting the roads
will lead me to where
i'm supposed to be.

i'm reminded that time keeps going.
and one year from now will come so fast
even though right now it feels so far.
one year from now has so much potential
to be all i've ever wanted and more.
one year from now
soon will be knocking at the door.
am i doing what it takes to welcome
it with eagerness instead of dread?
i want to let one year from now in.

i'll tell you,
no worries
when you say something
that doesn't sit right with me.
and instead of noticing
that i don't actually mean it
you tell me that i'm *so easy to please*.

the sun came out to play.
the temperature was just
where it needed to be.
the coffee tasted better.
the conversations were easy.
simple things showing up beautifully.

you're the main character
everyone wants to be.
and i've never met anyone
who owns who they are
so unapologetically.
and i wonder how you
cannot care so effortlessly
and be ok with no one understanding
who you want to be.
you move with the wind and never worry
about an unexpected turn of events
because you trust it was supposed to happen
to get you where you need to be next.
you're one in a million and not in a cheesy way
because nothing about you is simple or overdone.
you're the rare one.

when i was deep in it
i would've done anything
for it to be over.
and now that i've been
removed from it for so long
all i feel is nostalgia
for an unappreciated
moment in time.

don't let them steal your joy.
wear your favorite outfit
for the third time this week.
keep talking about your hobby
that brings happiness.
order whatever you're truly
wanting on the menu.
when you let go of the idea
that you need to do things
in a way to please other people,
you find freedom to be yourself.

some flowers just aren't meant to bloom
and you may never know why.
even if you did everything right.
some flowers just weren't for this time.

my biggest fear
is never being able
to stand on my own.
my biggest fear
is being alone.
what if it's just me at the end of it all?
would i be there for myself if i fall?

no one is making me
happy birthday shout outs
on facebook or instagram.
a collage of memories
from parties,
lake days,
late night movies,
and sunsets.
and i'm not sure
if i'd even want them.
i feel so invisible to the world
and hell, even to me.
i'm not sure if i even want to be seen.
maybe that is why i've yet
to get *best* put before *friend*
when talking about me,
because i'm too complicated
and messy.

this september will be different.
i won't hold on to things
that need to be let go.
i won't be afraid of being too bold.
i won't allow myself to compare my season
to all the seasons ahead of me.
i will go into this september differently.

i held you for a minute
in the grand scheme of things.
i blinked and you were gone.
never to be seen.
it was only just a moment.
so small it almost wasn't.
but i can't stop thinking
of what would've happened
if you were more than just a blink of the eye
and instead,
were all my eyes got to see
until the end of time.

i see you in the sunrays on august days
when you should have been here with me.
i wonder who you are now.
i wonder what you have seen.
there is so much unknown
surrounding you.
i wonder if we would act like strangers
who don't even recognize each other in town.
or if in that moment we would intertwine
and have a go at it this time around.

today my favorite song came on.
the one you told me was lame
as you skipped to the next.
this time i turned it up louder,
because it was just me
and i'm in the driver's seat now.
not a passenger
that has no control of the ride.

how do i keep moving forward
while you are paused in a past
that i just want to keep
rewinding back to?

maybe all of these trials
i've met along the way
have paved a path
for someone else
to not have to experience all of this pain.
or at the very least,
let them know
they aren't alone along the way.

i'm not afraid to get dirt under my nails
or run barefoot down the street.
i'm not afraid to pick wildflowers
on the side of the road
as i jump a fence or two along the way.
i'm not afraid of spilling
some waffle batter on the kitchen floor
or getting a little syrup in my hair.
because at the end of it all
i want the memories attached
to the messy moments.
the moments i simply didn't care.

what if tomorrow
i got to start over brand new?
would i embrace the fresh start?
would i live the life
i have always tried to pursue?

there are sunsets
that i won't forget.
the way everything was golden
and nothing mattered
but the space between us,
and what we did in the moments
it took to close those gaps.
i want to stay here forever
because where it's golden
nothing else matters
but soaking it in.

the sun coming up over the horizon
is filled with hope
of an untouched today.
there's never a better time than right now
to believe that things will be ok.

i'm healing for us.
i want the best for you,
but also,
me too.
give you the start
i never got
while healing
the inner child in me
with you.

there's beauty
in catching the sunrise
with only your eyes.
it's just a small moment in time.
it's meant to be brief
but genuinely appreciated.
like a lot of things in life.

there are hills worth climbing
for <u>more than just the view</u>.
<u>think of what all the trails</u>
<u>could teach you.</u>

i want more peaceful mornings.
a cup of coffee with room for cream.
sunlight starting
to peak through the windows.
fresh out of the shower feeling.
i want more moments
that calm my soul and help me find peace.
there's something about a slow morning
that makes me at ease.

when i nurture myself
instead of over consuming
other people's lives,
oh, the garden that blooms out of me.
oh, the beauty i find.

what i would give
to actually be as calm
as people think that i am.
they have no idea
all the intrusive thoughts
living in my head.

i'm healing myself first,
so i don't project
my struggles onto you.
i want you to carry no burden
of what i've gone through.

december holds so much.
the end of the best times,
or what was needed to come to an end.
december has hints of hope
for what is to come.
it has closure for all that was lost.
december is a heavy and hopeful month.

the thing is,
i've never wished you ill.
i just could no longer wish you for me
while you were wishing on someone
that i couldn't be.

i've let go of what's not
serving me,
like leaves in the wind.
they had their season,
but i'm moving forward
with new growth and
good reason.

i didn't lose myself
when i welcomed you in.
i got to share
all the things i loved
and longed to give to
more than just myself.
while getting to be loved
by someone else.

yes, there may be hurt
that comes along the way.
but you hurt because you love so much.
and love is so much better to feel than hate.

today i'll be just five percent
more present than i was yesterday.
and five percent more the day after that.
i slowly realized all i was missing out on
by thinking too far into the future
or dwelling too long on the past.
the present moment is really all i have,
so i'll be here a little more now.

take more deep breaths.
sit and listen to your heart beat.
watch your hair blow in the wind.
put your bare feet in the grass.
you are here.
you are an amazing soul
that deserves to know
just how much you are needed,
just how much you existing is world changing.

you shouldn't feel guilty
for feeling joy alongside the pain.
that's grieving.
it comes in waves.

this month will be better than the last.
a fresh start.
a new beginning.
an opportunity to start the habits i have left
waiting in the corner collecting dust.
i'll wash my face more.
i'll move my body with the wind.
i'll sit without any distractions.
i'll do my best to make this month
better than the last.
and if i don't this time around,
i always have the next.

anxiety feels like
that awkward moment in time
when you are walking toward someone
and you're getting closer and closer
to each other.
trying not to make eye contact too early.
maybe looking at your phone.
maybe looking to your left.
you know you're about to get there,
but you haven't quite yet.
closer and closer you close the gap.
until you intersect
and say hi with a small smile
for a moment.
and now you can breathe a sigh of relief
that it's over.

the pour down rain days
and the ones filled with sun rays,
are what have gotten me to this place.
the rain has taught me to <u>slow down</u>
<u>and take deep breaths</u>.
the sun has given me
<u>my confidence and depth</u>.

there is chaos here
in this messy in-between.
the upriver battle.
the lost at sea.
but what these waters have taught me
i wouldn't trade for a thing.

i will not do things anymore
to make other people happy
while it simultaneously pains me.
i spent years only doing things
that would leave people pleased.
i will own the fact
that i'm brutally honest
and true to myself.
because i deserve it after
being walked all over for so long.

when i find myself wondering
what life would look like
if i'd taken the other path,
i remind myself
that it was never
meant for me to travel
even if it may be better if i knew.
it wasn't a part of my story
to see that route through.

tell that person you love them.
say yes to the exciting opportunity
you are nervous about.
talk to the person
you haven't reached out to in awhile
but keep saying you will soon.
make that call.
say that yes.
love and let go of that grudge.
savor the now.
sitting in *what if* land is the worst feeling.
tomorrow is only a thought
not a guarantee.

this is the season of healing.
book an appointment with that therapist.
buy that solo plane ticket to the city
you've wondered about.
write a letter to your past self.
this is the season of healing
for you and no one else.

there is comfort in the consistency
that peeks through the chaos.

as the seasons change,
the two of us grow together.
through the worst and the best
of weather.

you don't need a new year to start over.
to become what you've wanted to be.
to go after that dream.
there is march and april.
there is october and november.
or any month in-between.
don't feel like you missed your shot.
waiting until january is mainstream.

they say it takes two months
until a new habit is formed with ease.
so why am i on month ten
of this new life without you
and all i can do is continue to grieve?
i don't want to form a life
where you aren't here
to take part in all of the little in-betweens.

color coordinated closets,
kept up calendars,
and saturday plans
made the monday before,
aren't my thing.
i'm a wandering soul
that needs freedom
to move as i please.

they will say,
ask and you shall receive.
but don't take that lightly.
because what you put out into the universe
over and over again
has a way of showing up
when you least expect it.

i think we both knew that the sun setting
wouldn't be where this ended.
we knew that in just a short amount of time
the sun would rise and we would realize
that we would never see another sunset again
without knowing the other is watching.

the last few seasons
have been hard and dreary,
but i hope you are ready
for a season filled with happiness
and golden sun.
you deserve it more than anyone.

i want more days
that feel like coming home
and putting on the clothes
that comfort me.
nuzzling in my favorite spot on the couch
with lavender tea.
escaping into a book
with a story so different than mine.
i need these small cozy moments in life.

the person i was five years ago
would probably have been
intimidated by who i am today,
but she shouldn't be.
it took years of built-up pain.
hills conquered.
races run.
to get to a place
where i could know who i truly was.

don't be afraid to laugh too loud,
eat the last slice of pizza someone offers,
or pick the playlist in the car.
don't be afraid to take what others
are offering if you want it.
don't feel like you have to keep saying,
no that's ok.
because you know you actually want to say,
ok, thanks!
don't be afraid to be bold here.
things can go your way.

i watered my garden
until it was full and over-growing.
some people couldn't handle
all that bloomed from me
and how much nourishing myself
changed who i used to be.
but i'm sitting back now
and enjoying my new scenery.
because i did it only for me.

i hope for more mornings
that are slow and beautiful
and remind me that being here
is a miracle.

i know the winters bring days
that turn dark too soon,
but even the sun needs rest too.
it's hard to always be the light
for everyone while also being it for you.

on the days when i wonder
when the clouds will part.
when the rain will be put on pause.
when the golden sun will peak out.
i find comfort in knowing
that life changing moments
can be right around the corner.

last year i didn't think
i'd make it to this place
where i'd wake up
without my pulse running a full race.
but here i am,
365 days later,
the steadiest i've ever been.
oh, what a year of healing can do.

i want more core memory days.
the ones where i remember
every detail.
down to the feeling
of the clothes i wore
and the smells i inhaled.

today give yourself
a little more grace.
you are navigating unpaved roads
and hikes with no clear signs.
give yourself a little more grace.
don't forget all of your victorious climbs.

you are the sun and the stars.
the moon and the waves.
and you being here's just as important
as the air we breathe.

let us fill the world
with sentences that flow
with compliments
and kind gestures.
let us be quicker to tell someone
all of their rights instead of their wrongs.
let us heal together through this all.

my act of kindness would be
to make sure no one felt alone at sea.
to have the support they think is long gone.
to give them the guidance
to make it back
to where they belong.

the earth has season changes
to heal and grow.
and the same goes for you.
don't feel bad for rebuilding
and letting go.

there are gardens in you
ready to bloom.
they are just waiting for you
to weed out what's weighing you down
and make room.

i apologize to my body,
my mind,
and my soul
for making you feel
so bad and alone.
i hope you can forgive me
for what i said on my journey
of figuring out what self-love was.
i was hurting.

rain comes quietly and quickly.
or loud and never ending.
and why does that
feel the same way for
the negative thoughts in my head?

i hold my breath
in most every situation these days.
somehow it feels like when things
are going more than ok,
that waves will come crashing in.
lightning and thunder all around.
i wish i could just enjoy
all the beautiful moments
without worrying about
if my feet will be taken out
from under the ground.

you don't need to move
at such a rushed pace.
there are flowers
worth stopping
to smell along the way.
and strangers
worth talking to
about their day.
don't forget to look up
every now and then
to enjoy all the things
in this present moment.

i'm not looking for perfection.
i like wrinkles in my sheets.
coffee stains on the side of my mugs.
my hair a little wind-blown.
i like things a little messy.
i like things well loved.

don't wish away the season.
watch the leaves change
while they are here.
catch the snowflakes
while they fall.
watch the flowers bloom
while they grow.
feel the hot sun
while it's out.
you don't want to wish away
the beauty in the now.

i'll call a rainy day
comfy and cozy
when it's just one day.
but if it stays any longer
my mind feels gray.
my to-do list gets left in the dust.
i sit and wonder
how time moved
but i didn't.
and slowly that is how the storm comes.

don't hold back the compliments.
the i love you's.
the good news.
don't hold back on the things
that can help heal old wounds.

i love sunsets in april
because there is hope in sight
that the light will turn back on
for a longer time.

clouds with shades of grays.
night is an early riser
and longer it stays.
outside time is limited from frigidness
and lack of movement.
it's no wonder seasonal depression
always has a way of make itself known
when everything turns cold.

i want more days
where my outfit
makes me feel most like myself.
and my mind doesn't
wander anywhere else.
i want more days where i sit and listen
instead of hurry and talk.
and days where my happiness
isn't tied to how efficiently
i move with the clock.

i find comfort in the genuine people.
the ones who never leave you
questioning where you stand.
the ones who tell it like it is,
but with love.
because with genuine people
you never feel like you have a relationship
that is true only to you,
but something else to them
without you knowing.

i'll start my week with promise,
but be forgiving when things
don't go as planned.
there are unexpected events
that require patience and grace
you didn't know you needed in place
on monday.

i'm in the driver seat of my life,
but i don't get the official map.
just an idea of where i might go
if i stay on this road.
how exciting it is
to think of all the possibilities
ahead of me
that i don't even know are exactly
what i need.

i found so much peace within myself
that no matter the lack of nourishment
from other people,
i can still stand just as tall on my own.
i'll take the compliments with gratitude,
but i don't need them
to be proud of who i am.

i'm starting with healing myself first
because it's the only control i have
to go from there and then
lend a helping hand.

today i'll pick up my home.
clean the corners of her i've never seen.
take inventory of what she needs.
make her feel whole again.
apologize for the lack of effort.
but i know she is forgiving,
because she's the only one who understands
just how hard i'm trying
even on the days when it feels like
i don't care at all.

i battle with wanting
to prove you wrong,
or giving in and saying
you were right all along.

don't forget who you are at the core
when you find yourself in a place
that is trying to get you to be
who you've never wanted to be.
it is more than ok to have boundaries.

life is a lot of unknowns
intertwined with hopeful plans.
so i'm choosing to anticipate the best
instead of the worst.
i'd much rather be pleasantly surprised
by all the good happening in my life.

there's nothing wrong
with moving on
and closing doors
to places that built you
but serve you no more.

it's ok to be uncomfortable
as the seasons change
and you aren't ready.
it's ok to wonder
about the weather ahead.
but i hope you know
you can change with the seasons
in a way that works for you.
take it slow.
ease yourself in.
you're so much more capable of being
adaptable than you realize right now.

i stopped sharing my dreams
with people who only dream
when they sleep.

you turned the pages of me so gently
and i knew in that moment
i'd let you know my full story
without question.
because you were someone who
paused between pages and listened,
instead of being someone who only
skimmed me and missed the best parts.

i'll meet you at sunrise-
because it always does.
and you never have to wonder
if it's going to come.
even if it's covered with clouds
the sun will come out.
and i want you to know
i will do the same for you
without a doubt.

i'll love you no matter the roads you take
that i don't understand,
because i'm believing that you know
why you're taking that way
even if it's a journey i'd never take.
it isn't my place to judge the way you have
chosen to go about your drive.
it's your life.

i have endless forgiveness
for my own inner peace.
wishing you the best,
but i'm not letting your negativity
take space in my mind.
i'm so protective of the healing
i have done inside.

maybe the roads
are calling you back
to a place you thought
you wanted nothing to do with.
maybe it just wasn't the right time
and now these roads
are exactly where you need to be
in order to keep up with
where you are trying to go in life.

there are strangers
that know more about me
than you do.
and while it used to bother me,
i've realized now
that it doesn't matter
how close we should be.
if you only want to know
the surface level version of me,
that's who you will get
and that's no one's loss but your own.

you're glowing like the sun.
you're laughing and having fun.
healing looks so good on you.

i'll protect my secrets
and my heart
from everyone except you.
because you can see right through me
and i let you.

today, open all the windows.
let the fresh air in.
the sound of the wind,
a car passing,
and a bird chirping.
today, let in the glimpses
of present moments.

the stars don't listen
when someone tells them
to stop shinning so bright.
so why are you letting other people
dim your light?

i'm no longer hard on myself
for my past mistakes.
all i can do is pack up the experiences
and carry them with me along the way.
a reminder of how much i've gone through
and still forgave myself
for what i didn't know then.
because what i didn't know then
is the blue print of what
i'm able to know now moving forward.

they'll call it a coincidence or luck,
but i believe in seeing it
as blessings from a dream
that i wasn't quick to give up.

everyone deserves a person
that encourages their spark.
the first one to hear the good news.
the first one you cry to.
the one who never questions
their late-night knock at the door.
the one who never questions
sleeping on their floor.
everyone deserves a person
that's there unconditionally.

i'll never quite understand
how rain can fall while the sun is out.
all i can guess is that
it's the earth's way of showing us
how it feels to heal through pain.
that sadness can be met with hopefulness
and that's more than ok.

meet me at golden hour.
where everything is softer for a while.
people stop in awe and wonder.
time here is limited,
so it is cherished.
come feel the magic here
where for a moment
the light touches us all.

meet me at golden hour

to read more work by jennae cecelia,
check out her other ten books:

healing for no one but me

the sun will rise and so will we

the moon will shine for us too

losing myself brought me here

dear me at fifteen

i am more than my nightmares

uncaged wallflower- extended edition

i am more than a daydream

uncaged wallflower

bright minds empty souls

about the author

www.JennaeCecelia.com

@JennaeCecelia on Instagram

@JennaeCecelia on TikTok

jennae cecelia is a best-selling author
of inspirational poetry books
and is best known for her books,
the sun will rise and so will we
and *uncaged wallflower*.

she is also an inspirational speaker
who digs into topics like
self-love, self-care, mental health,
and body positivity.

her mission is to encourage people
to reach their full potential and
live a life filled with positivity and love.

meet me at golden hour

Made in the USA
Columbia, SC
08 May 2023

16198435R00071